Miss Piggy's

TREASURY *of* ART MASTERPIECES

from the
Kermitage Collection

Henry Beard
Archivist & Editor

Michael K. Frith
Curator of the Collection

John E. Barrett
Photographer of the Exhibits

A Jim Henson Muppet Presentation

Holt, Rinehart and Winston
New York

*To Frank Oz, one of my oldest and cherest friends,
who has so often given moi a helping hand in my career—this book
is thoughtfully dedicated.**

Copyright © 1982, 1983, 1984 by Henson Associates, Inc.
Miss Piggy, Muppet Press, Muppets, and character names are trademarks of Henson Associates, Inc.
All rights reserved, including the right to reproduce this
book or portions thereof in any form.
Published by Holt, Rinehart and Winston,
383 Madison Avenue, New York, New York 10017.
Published simultaneously in Canada by Holt, Rinehart and
Winston of Canada, Limited.

Library of Congress Cataloging in Publication Data
Main entry under title:
Miss Piggy's treasury of art masterpieces from the
Kermitage collection.
1. Art—Private collections—Caricatures and cartoons.
2. American wit and humor, Pictorial.   I. Frith,
Michael K.   II. Beard, Henry.   III. Barrett, John E.
NC1763.A66M57   1984   702′.07   84-10939

ISBN 0-03-000743-7
First Edition

Designer: Marc Cheshire
Printed in the United States of America
1 3 5 7 9 10 8 6 4 2

*And to Kermie, who I am going to mention in this teensy tootsie note, even though he asked me not to. He also asked me not to call my collection the Kermitage, because he said he had really done nothing to deserve it (which isn't true; he helped a lot, particularly in getting the pictures to hang straight), and why didn't I call it something else, like the Moitropolitan Collection or the Museum of Moidern Art—I mean, give moi une break, frog! Actually, though, the fact is that the little dear is too shy and retiring. He reminds me of that artist Somerset Gauguin, who went off to Tahiti and spent all his time painting screwy pictures of Polynesians when he could have been a hotshot in Paris, France. Y'know, Kermie paints too, though I do think he uses too much green, and really Claudie (Monet to you) does better lily pads, if you want moi's honest opinion. But it would be just like Kermit to slip off to some dessert island like Tutti-Frutti, though I don't know what you could paint there. After all, just look at the masterpieces in this book—the key to great art is great clothes, and they don't wear any nice ball gowns or ermine stoles or sequined capes in les tropics. In fact, they don't wear anything, they're just stark naked...well, listen here, Mr. Froguin, if you plan to skip town with your paintbox and go to some place where the drinks have little umbrellas stuck in them and lounge around all day in those nice madras shorts I bought you but you never wear, strumming a ukulele and doing risquay portraits of boola-boola dancers in the buff, you've got another thing coming. Of all le gall! Here I go out of my way to give you a plug in my book, and this is the thanks I get. Artists! Yucque!

ISBN 0-03-000743-7

Contents

Introduction
A Few Words from the Directoire
of the Kermitage

Moi has always been a mavenne of les arts, and whenever I have had a day or two free from my busy schedule as an international superstar, I have scoured hotsy-totsy palazzos and snazzy châteaus, shopping for priced-less artworks by old masteurs. I have also checked out hundreds of tag sales, flea markets, charity bazaars, and sales de rummage, because you never know when you are going to run across a Van Goya or an El Fresco with a five-dollar price tag on it between a pile of left-handed galoshes and a boxful of jelly jars. The result of my tireless search for dynamite art treaseurs is an eye-popping assemblage of cream de la crop brique-a-braque that various critiques have been kind enough to call "unbelievable," "indescribable," and "simply staggering."

Those few fortunate individuals who have been given a private tour of moi's lush but tasteful gallery have all cautioned me not to show my collection to the public—obviously they are concerned about the problem of theft—but I feel that I have an obligation to the world at large to throw open the doors of the Kermitage, so de speak, and give my millions of fans a once-in-une-lifetime opportunity to view a few of the masterpieces of painting and sculpture I have glommed on to during my many years of collecting. The fourteen museum pieces reproduced in this lavish book were chosen from among

the many classic objects de art obtained by me from penniless counts and down-in-le-mouth dukes in fancy foreign places. But do not worry, chère art loveur, there are no boring Greek flowerpots, no spooky old mummies in esophaguses, no dopey pictures of disappointing fruit snacks, no weird paintings of silos with propellers on them by old Dutch twerps, and no ugly heaps of metal junk made by some goofball with a blowtorch. And there are no chintzy copies, either. All of the portraits are signed by the artist, often with a personal message to moi from the painteur himself (the one from Mr. Picasso is particularly nice), and all of the statues have the name of the chiseler on them.

Being a connoisseurette is a demanding and solitary occupation, and of course if there are any awards for Curatorix of the Month or Best Supporteur of the Arts, or something like that, I alone must bear the responsibility of traveling to a glamorous but distant city to accept it and make a little speech and pose for the photographeurs. Nevertheless, I would be remiss if I did not take a moment to mention moi's special art adviser, the noted dealeur Mr. B. Bernard "Bernie" Bernhardt Bernier Bernardi (Europeans certainly do have a lot of names!), who has been kind enough to write a short introduction to this teensy book of mine. He was of enormous help to me in amassing this fabulous collection, and he always encouraged moi to be a bold and fearless col-lecteur. I remember, when he showed me a remarkable bust of a Venetian dodge by Pi-nocchio (I didn't like it—it looked like Gonzo, only worse), which he happened to find in a little shop off Canal Street in Ven-ice, that he said, "In art, one must never be afraid to forge ahead." He is a man who has the courage of his convictions, and an associ-ate of his once told me that he has many, many convictions. His services are much in demand—he is wanted all over the place—and I am grateful that he was able to take me in and show me all his latest discoveries and advise me on major purchases, even though it was a bit inconvenient to meet him in all those funny empty warehouses in Brooklyn and coffee shops along the New Jersey Turnpike.

And now, if moi may give vous an itsy-bitsy piece of advice, as you peruse this mag-nificent book, don't turn down the corners of the pages and don't make thumb smootches on the prints. This volume is cer-tain to be a collecteur's item itself in the years to come, and I know that you would hate to have a copy with a bad case of ear du dog. And by le way, if you just happen to come across some ratty old painting in your attique that is just taking up valuable space, and it's signed by some minor unimportant unknown famous person like, say, Massag-gio or Fellini, do let moi know, won't vous?

Ta-ta!

Foreword

by B. Bernard "Bernie" Bernhardt Bernier Bernardi,
Dealer in Fine Arts and Adviser to the Kermitage Collection

IT gives me great pleasure to write this foreword for my dear friend and esteemed client—mein Liebchen, mon amie, cara mio—Miss Piggy. Although, to the best of my knowledge and belief, I have no recollection of the circumstances of our first meeting, or of any alleged transactions that may or may not have taken place at that time, I shall never forget the profound love of art reflected in those extraordinary blue eyes, eyes that reminded me of the azure skies of my native Italy. Here, I knew, was a collector with passion, and such a person, I may assure you, mein bon amigo, is not born every minute, no matter what you may have heard. I felt at once a mysterious itching, tingling sensation in the palms of my hands, and I realized in an instant that she and I had what the old glockenspiel players in the Swiss village where I was born called simply "the good vibrations." And if I was later able to bring to her attention a number of unusual artworks, it was only because of this special bond between us and a sensitivity to the mind of the creative genius acquired in my youth in my homeland of Austria, when I myself dabbled in painting and sculpture—a sensitivity that permits me almost to feel, when in the presence of certain great artworks, that I was there when the artist painted them.

I am not sure what impelled me from the very beginning of my life to become involved in the fine arts. Maybe I absorbed a fascination with beauty from the limpid air of my birthplace, that magical landscape of Provence. However, I do know that, somewhere in the depths of my soul, I longed for the chance to find what we in the art world call "a live one," that is, a great patron with taste and vision whom I could assist in the accumulation of a collection that would be second to none. Was that foolish pride? Perhaps. After all, we Bavarians are known for our vanity. And surely it would be vain of me to suggest, state, aver, or otherwise represent in any way, shape, form, or fashion that I, or any agent of mine, was in any way personally responsible for the creation of the Kermitage. For although I may have occasionally advised Miss Piggy on a purchase—and I do not recall at this time having done so—it is truly she who must receive all the credit for having created this astonishing treasure house of masterpieces.

I congratulate Miss Piggy on this stupendous accomplishment, and although current circumstances compel me to abandon, for the time being, my modest calling as a dealer in rarities and collectables, I will always feel richer in a very real sense for having known this remarkable benefactress of the arts.

Bernie
Kennedy Airport
March 1984

Thomas Gainsborough. *Green Boy.*

WELCOME to our little tour of the Kermitage. Are you wearing comfy shoes? Good. Now, as we climb Le Grand Staircase and pass into the Corridor of Culture, we immediately come upon a truly great work of genius, this dynamite portrait of a handsome, debonair young amphibian by the English artist Gainsborough. (Pronunciation, I feel, is a matteur of personal taste, but just for the record, I say Gainsbo-RUFF.) Moi asks vous, is this not a masterpiece? Such delicate paintulosity, such deft brushification, and such a brilliant choice of subject! Note the bold use of color, particularly green, and the subtle interplay of light and shadow and frog. Note also the nifty hat (*see detail*). Although the eighteenth century was marked by a depressing lack of hair driers and lip gloss, one must admit that the duds were extremely snappy.

THOMAS GAINSBOROUGH. Green Boy. *Oil on canvas. After 1787. Purchased from the collection of the Earl of Gatwick at his family estate, "Heathrow," using funds generously provided by a benefactor who wishes to remain anonymous and his nephew, Robin. Signed "Thomas Gainesburgh" (crossed out); "Thomas Ganesboro" (crossed out); "Thomas Gainsborough!"*

Henri de Toulouse-Lautrec. *La Belle Epigue.*

WE are now entering the Rotunda of Prints, Drawings, and Scribbles. Frankly, I've gone light on this stuff in my collection. I don't know about you, but I am bored stiffe by black-and-white sketches of crumbly old temples that no one has bothered to keep up, or smudgy doodles of some funny-looking gizmo used to press prunes or fling big rocks at castles. But moi does like colorful posteurs, and one of my favorites is this one by the extremely short French artist, Toulouse-Lautrec (José Ferrer played the part in the movie—*Lust for Height,* I think it was called). With a simple but dramatic composition and just a few dibs and dabs of bright color, he has captured the stunning beauty of a glamorous superstar at the famous Moulin Frogue in Montmartre—a blonde bombshell who, I must say, bears a striking resemblance to me, though moi would never be caught dead in those clunky clodhoppeurs (*see detail*).

HENRI DE TOULOUSE-LAUTREC. La Belle Epigue. *Polychrome xerograph. Before 1985. Recent acquisition from the Going Out of Business Gallery, made possible by a onetime grant from the Teensy Drawer in the Tippy-Top of the Bureau. Signed and numbered (320/100) and accompanied by the original mailing tube with French stamps on it.*

James A. McNeill Whistler. *Arrangement in Gray and Black with Creep (Whistler's Weirdo).*

MANY visitors to the Kermitage ask moi why I have this thing hanging on the wall here. Well, first, an important connoisseuse such as moiself has an obligation to display significant works of art, however revolting, so that fellow vultures de culture (such as vous) can enjoy a wide range of visual treats, from le best to les pits. Second, it was free. And third, it's hanging here because there is a big splotch on the wall from the time when the bath overflowed upstairs while I was giving my little Fou-Fou a shampoo, and the cute darling jumped out of the tub and ran off and moi had to chase her, and I left the water running, and it leaked right down, and I just couldn't have a stain the size of an omelette right here in the middle of the Salon of the Greats and Not-So-Greats. Come to think of it, though, it was a rather nice sort of spot—very abstract, with a powerful counterpoint of browns and yellows. It does seem sort of a pity to cover it up. By le way, I *did* try hanging this upside down, and it's not much better (*see detail*).

JAMES ABBOTT MCNEILL WHISTLER. Arrangement in Gray and Black with Creep (Whistler's Weirdo). *Oily substance on tablecloth. $18.72 (with tax). Unsolicited gift (left in coatroom). Available for immediate acquisition by interested individual or institution. $17.95? Signed "Jimmie Abie Mac Whistler." Complete with Luminart 40-watt brass painting light. $14.95?*

Auguste Rodin. *The Smooch.*

As we pass through the Gossiping Gallery and enter the Court of the Classy Sculptures, our gaze is immediately drawn to this unforgettable portrayal, in rare cat's-eye marble, of a pair of young loveurs locked in a passionate embrace. The first thing we notice about this sculpture is that the beautifully carved figures—a demure pig maiden and her one true frog—have all their arms and legs (*see detail*), which is something you can't say about a lot of the statues in even the best collections. The problem with so many museums is that so much of the stuff in them is so *old.* I don't know how vous feel about it, but whenever I hit a room full of busted rocks with squiggles on them or half a torseau of some Greek armwrestleur looking like he's posing for an underwear ad, I just breeze right through and head for the gift shop. And speaking of gift shops, unlike many underequipped museums, the Kermitage has seven of them.

AUGUSTE RODIN. The Smooch. *Sculpted block of lobby marble. 1886 (lbs.). Commissioned from the artist by the Kermitage Collection and acquired on the layaway plan using funds from the Garment Foundation. Signed "A Rodin" and inscribed "To Miss Piggy, one swell gal, from Gus, Michael, Angelo, and all the guys at the studio."*

Leonardo da Vinci. *Mona Moi.*

LEAVING the Court of the Classy Sculptures, we see the entrance to the Talkitorium, where moi gives little lectures and slide shows on important art subjects, like "Collecting Rare Pieces of Kung-Fu Throwing China from the Fling Dynasty" and "How to Get Those Nasty Stains Out of Old Stained Glass." Just ahead is the Grand Room de la Best du Best, where one of the world's most adored paintings hangs in solitary splendeur. I have this knockout artwork way back here by itself because, frankly, many low de brow persons just zip into the Kermitage to give this masterpiece a quick look-see, and I want them to be exposed to as much art as possible on the way. This painting is sometimes called the *Giaconda Smile,* and I think this is because the very attractive model seems to be saying, "*Gee, I kinda* hope Mr. da Vinci wraps this portrait up pronteau, because my cheeks are getting all moobly trying to hold this stupid smile." I also want to mention in passing that although the reproductions in this book don't show it, each of my paintings is mounted in a very snazzy frame, and the one that came with this one is, I feel, a particularly superb example of the framifier's art (*see detail*).

LEONARDO DA VINCI. Mona Moi. *Acrylic on fiberboard. Around 1503. Acquired by cash purchase from a mysterious and reclusive private collector's hoard of fine art in a locker at the Port Authority Bus Terminal. Additional acquisitions at the same time included the menu for the last supper and the fabulous da Vinci phone books. Signed "the one, the only—the great da Vinci" and dated "circa 1503."*

Hans Holbein. *Jester at the Court of Henry VIII.*

As we stand here in the Atrium of Some Other Artworks, let us take a moment or two to learn how to look at a painting. How *not* to look at a painting is to rent one of those bulky tape recorders and listen to some tiresome fud-de-duddy blather on about messytints or Gothic dipstychs or how Luigi Fettucini was one of the pre-Ralphites because he did all his pictures in goulash. You must make up your own mind. Stand in front of the picture and check it out. If it's something nice, like this picture of a bear, you might nod and remark, "Well executed, bearistically speaking," and then say something a teensy bit nit-picky about a detail no one else is looking at (*see detail*), such as, "Of course, Garbaggio's bananas have more bananisity." But if it's something dumb, like a picture of a bunch of chubby little brats with wings on their backs fanning a fat lady in a bedsheet, frown slightly and say, "I think the artist showed a better mastery of Rocococulation during his lavender period, don't vous?" Then head for the gift shop.

HANS HOLBEIN. Jester at the Court of Henry VIII. *Greasepaint on canvas flat. 1539? Long-term loan from the Ufozzi Gallery of the Accomedia Museum in Venice, California, in exchange for Michael and Angelo's "Cream Pieta." Signed "Joannes Holpenius, artistus terrificus" and inscribed on the back "Actus Unus, Scenus Duus—Ursus Ridiculus."*

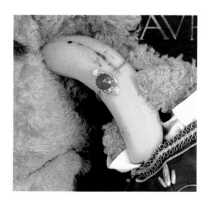

Jan van Eyck. *The Marriage of Froggo Amphibini and Giopiggi Porculini.*

ENTERING the Great Hall of the Fabulous Masterpieces, we come upon this magnificent depictulation of the wedding of a merchant frog and a lovely pig princess. One must examine works of art such as this very closely, because sometimes they have hidden meanings. This particular portrait is just chock-full of symbols: the open window symbolizes light, air, and bugs; the candle stands for birthdays, nice little restaurants, and power failures; the gloves and jewel on the hands of the bride (who symbolizes beauty, intelligence, and talent) suggest supremely good taste; the cute pooch stands for adorableness and small messes; and the slippeurs on the floor (which symbolizes flatness, waxy buildup, and itsy-bitsy dust balls) stand for shoes. Frankly, moi does not know what the weird little ear net symbolizes (*see detail*). This may be one of those cases where you're supposed to spot what is wrong with the picture, like finding all the horses with horns on their heads in those ratty French tapestries.

JAN VAN EYCK. The Marriage of Froggo Amphibini and Giopiggi Porculini. *Cheese tempera on ⅜" plywood. 1??4. Purchased from the artist's great-great-great-great-great-great-great grandson, Mr. Jan van Eyck XI of Allenwood, Pennsylvania. Signed by the artist and inscribed "To Miss Piggy" in bold* markeur magique *calligraphy.*

Sandro Botticelli.
The Birth of You Know Who.

As we proceed down the Great Hall, we encounter another Fabulous Masterpiece. Many paintings of the Italian Renaissance period illustrate dopey stories taken from mythology, such as how the goddess of mushy vegetables got mad at some silly floozy and turned her into a side order of succotash, or how some fathead had all the nasty stuff in the world, like sniffles and crows' feet and hangnails, locked up in a box, only she opened it and it all got out. But this one is much nicer—it shows Beauty, personified by a luscious pig deity, being wafted to shore by a pair of wind-bags scattering floweurs. There, she is greeted by an adoring frog (probably the god of umbrellas, hankies, and other handy things), who hands her a robe de

bath—a very handsome one, moi might add (*see detail*). I'm having a dress made just like it. Incidentally, the pig was worshipped as the epitome of grace and refinement throughout the ancient world except for a few places which, interestingly enough, were destroyed by volcanoes, earthquakes, and tidal waves.

SANDRO BOTTICELLI. The Birth of You Know Who. *Oil on drip-dry fabric. 1?82. Acquired at a garage sale held at the villa of the Duke of Jacuzzi along with a large lot of other important fourteenth-, fifteenth-, and sixteenth-century objects, including the famed Cellini flyswatter and Breughel's ice skates. Signed "Sandy Botticelli" and dated "early Renaissance."*

Edgar Degas. *The La Danseur.*

Leaving the Great Hall, we pass under the replica of the Porch of the Ladies Holding up the Roof with Their Heads and reenter the Court of the Classy Sculptures. Note the stunning blue-velvet backdrop (*see detail*). Here we find a darling bronze figure by Degas, a cute French artist noted for his simple, easy-to-spell name. I must say that a lot of people with very peculiar monikeurs ended up in the art biz. They really are quite a bother for the dedicated patronette of les arts. And while we are at it, so are all the dates in Roman numerals. It is so annoying in a museum not to know when the pictures were paintified because the sign on the wall has a bunch of D's and M's and X's and C's that look like someone sat on a typewriteur. And another thing. Bronze statues like this one are supposed to have been cast by some lost-wax process or other. Well, if they lost the stupid wax, what did they use—furniture polish? Shampoo? Cold cream? Let moi tell you, the study of art is no pique-nique.

EDGAR DEGAS. The La Danseur. *Hand-forged cast bronze with taffeta and pearls. 1893-ish. Acquisition by mail from the Museum of Finest Quality Stuff, Taipei, Taiwan. Engraved with the artist's signature, "Edgal Degas," and the place and approximate date of fabrication, "Palis, Flance, one big heck of a long time ago."*

Henri Rousseau. *The Sleepy Zootsy.*

AFTER departing from the Court of the Classy Sculptures, we pass the Closet of Uncatalogued Odds and Ends (we'll just leave that teensy door shut for now) and find ourselves once again in the Salon of the Greats and Not-So-Greats. I don't know how vous are holding up, but after a while I tend to get museumosis, and even with the wall-to-wall carpeting and all the conveniently placed candy machines here at the Kermitage, I find I just have to take a little break to avoid Art Overload. So while you eyeball this kooky picture—is this guy kidding???—I think I'll just nip over to the Veranda of the Foods of Many Nations for a quick nibble. Incidentally, I think this artist showed a better mastery of clothespressionism during his chartreuse period, and that, on the whole, Vowelaeioulo's vases had more jugulosity (*see detail*). What do vous think?

HENRI ROUSSEAU. The Sleepy Zootsy. *Airbrushed auto-body paint on metal van panel. 1897-VRG (N.J. plates). Traveling exhibition made possible through the generosity of the Parking Violations Department of the State of New Jersey. Signed "Hank the Crank Rousseau" and inscribed "Je dig le crazy hot jazz, yes no?"*

Rembrandt van Rijn. *Arisfroggle Contemplating the Bust of a Twerp.*

Here, at the end of the Salon of the Greats and Not-So-Greats, in the Niche of the Near Misses, hangs a very nice but flaky portrait of a philosopheur in a rather odd hat (*see detail*), looking at the head of a creep. Honestly, I think this painting would have been much more effective if the artist had shown this very distinguished frog looking at something a bit more appealing, like a cinderblock or a dish of prunes, or, better yet, if he was watching TV. You know, apropos de TV, you can have that ritzy museum look in your own home quite easily by picking up a few gold-painted picture frames of assorted sizes, pasting little labels on them, and hanging them over various objects in your house. For example, you could place one over your TV screen (*Après-Midi d'un Soap Opéra*), or your aquarium (*Les Fish*), or your microwave oven (*The Wreck of the Soufflé*). Afteur all, it is so important for each of us to have a little art in her daily life.

REMBRANDT VAN RIJN. Arisfroggle Contemplating the Bust of a Twerp. *Latex on polyester. ???0. Purchased from the personal collection of Prince Lieppe van Frogh of Waartdam, member of the royal House of Green. Signed "Rembrandt van Rijn" and personally authenticated by the artist with the inscription, "Thijs is nott a fjake!"*

Jan Vermeer. *Young Lady Adorning Herself with Pearls (and Why Not?).*

Hanging in the place of honor in the Salle des Goodies is this exquisite portrait of an even more exquisite woman adding the perfect final touches that make all the difference. Note the chic fur-bordered cape and the terrific pearls (*see detail*). Vous have to admit that people dressed better in les old days. I often think that moi would have enjoyed living in one of the nicer centuries, say the seventeenth, when people would lug you around in those comfy boxes with sticks on the ends, and knights were always putting their coats in puddles for you, but on the other hand, if you were a superstar such as myself, whenever you came out of a castle after a banquette, you'd be pestered by artists who wanted you to stand still for five hours while they painted your picture, and to give someone your autograph you had to chisel it on a rock or yank a feather off some bird's behind and go squeeze some berries for ink, and if you wished to call a friend on the phone, you had to use a pigeon, and then if someone called you while your pigeon was busy, you had to wait until it got back, and anyway you were probably always getting a wrong pigeon. Phooey.

JAN VERMEER. Young Lady Adorning Herself with Pearls (and Why Not?). *Eyeliner, mascara, and lacquer on chiffon. 1???. Discovered in Vermeer's condominium in Delft during remodeling, and purchased using funds from the deacquisition of an authentic 1964 DeSoto. Signed by the artist and dated "Tuesday."*

Grant Wood. *American Gothique.*

As we cross the Terrace of the Little Shrubs in Tubs, we pass the Center des Exhibitions, where I often hold temporary shows and retrospectives. Right now, we're closing up "Masterpieces of Cake Decoration" and getting set up for "Treasures of the World's Greatest Gift Shops." Just ahead is the American Wing. It's a bit torn up now because we're installing an early-twentieth-century soda fountain next to the nineteenth-century candy store, and we've had to move that perfectly restored ice cream truck over to the corner where we used to have the colonial cookie jars. Which is why this painting of a stalwart frog farmer and his noble wife is hanging here in the Vestibule of the Coats. I'll be honest with you. I'm not crazy about this picture. I think at the very least the artist could have painted them a nicer house and a little roadster so they could whiz into town for a movie once in a while. I do like the brooch, though (*see detail*).

GRANT WOOD. American Gothique. *Housepaint on roofing felt. 19??. Acquired at auction along with a large lot of unusual American pieces, including a Paul Revere bowling trophy, a Franklin toaster oven, several Navajo bath mats, a Tiffany sunlamp, a Frank Lloyd Wright birdhouse, and an Art Deco digital clock. Signed by the artist with his full name and social security number.*

Pablo Picasso. *Pig Before a Mirror.*

Now, as we reenter the Corridor of Culture, we end our little tour with this dramatique abstract painting of a pig standing in front of a very screwy mirror. Maybe it's a little goofy for you, but moi does like that dynamite wallpapeur (*see detail*). Believe it or not, many people dislike modern art because they don't understand what it is saying. This is silly. Modern art doesn't "say" anything, except maybe, "This is what happens when you put a big piece of canvas on the floor and knock a bucket of red paint on it from the top of a stepladder." It's also very easy to talk about intelligently. Just stand back and remark, "Quel globs and dribbles!" "What a masterful handling of the big swirls of blue goop!" And as a collector, you really only need to ask one question: Will it go with the sofa and the drapes?

PABLO PICASSO. Pig Before a Mirror. *Deck enamel on denim. 19?2. Purchased from Mr. Chico Picasso, the artist's brother, from the collection in his restaurant, "La Fonda del Food." Signed "Pablo Picasso." Also signed "Joe DiMaggio." Inscribed by the artist "From Pablo to my little gazpacho, Miss Piggy, olé, baby!"*

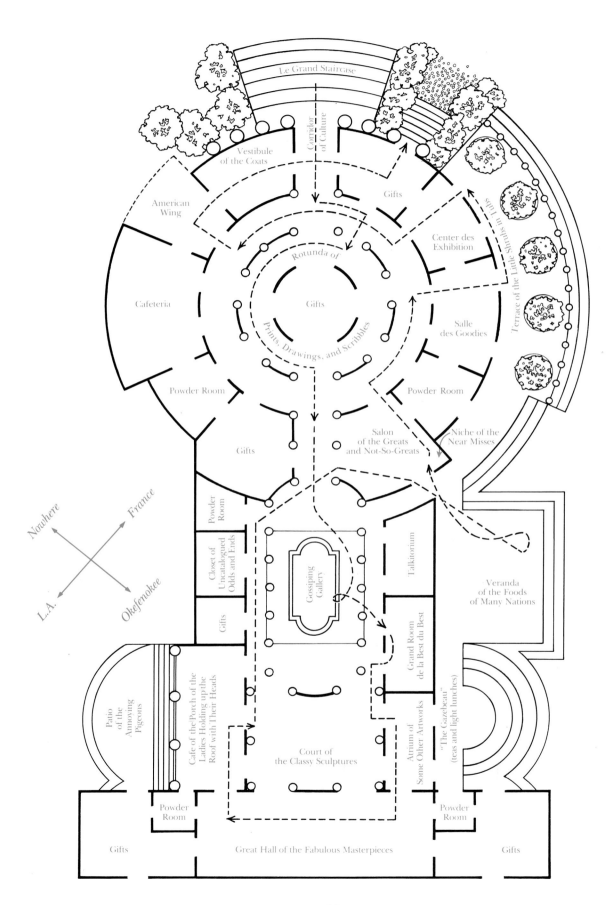

Le Grand Staircase

Vestibule
of the Coats

Corridor
of Culture

Gifts

American
Wing

Center des
Exhibition

Terrace of the Little Shrubs in Tubs

Cafeteria

Rotunda of

Gifts

Prints, Drawings, and Scribbles

Salle
des Goodies

Powder Room

Powder Room

Gifts

Salon
of the Greats
and Not-So-Greats

Niche of the
Near Misses

Nowhere

France

L.A.

Okefenokee

Powder
Room

Closet of Uncatalogued Odds and Ends

Gossiping
Gallery

Talkitorium

Veranda
of the Foods
of Many Nations

Gifts

Patio
of the
Annoying Pigeons

Cafe of the Porch of the Ladies Holding up the Roof with Their Heads

Grand Room
de la Best du Best

"The Gazebeau"
(teas and light lunches)

Court of
the Classy Sculptures

Atrium of
Some Other Artworks

Powder
Room

Powder
Room

Gifts

Great Hall of the Fabulous Masterpieces

Gifts

The Art of Collecting
by Miss Piggy, B. Lt., Msg.

I DO hope you enjoyed your "visit" to the Kermitage. I know that you were overwhelmed by moi's collection, and so I want to take a moment here, at the end du book, to assure you that you do not have to be a graduate of some double-dome academy like the Hudson River School in order to appreciate art. All you need to get started as a collecteur are supreme good taste, an eye for a bargain, and a few tricks of la trade that I will reveal to you. True, one does not become a great aficionadeau of the arts such as moi overnight, but you can begin to develop your aesthetique taste buds if you follow these few simple suggestions.

The first thing you must do is get rid of any horrid stuff you have hanging on your walls. *National Geographique* maps, creepy

(Fig. 1) Here is a plan de la floor of the galleries to give you an idea of the layout. Incidentally, for some reason art books always label their illustrations as figs. Who knows, maybe in les old days they got ink from the stupid things or mashed the skins into some kind of revolting paper. I wanted to label moi's illustrations plums or pineapples or something nice, but the publisheur simply would not go along, and since he gave in on the nice marbled papeur in the front and back of the book, I decided not to make too big a fuss about it. I admit I was just a teensy bit upset at that meeting, but his office was overdue for redecorating anyway.

gravestone rubbings, ratty kites, advertisements for movies in which moi did not star, posters of mean Spaniards in opera capes stabbing cattle—they all have to go. Be ruthless. Art and schlock do not mix.

Next, decide what you have room for. If you live in a hole-in-le-wall apartment, you might want to stick to ancient Roman dimes and quarters, porcelain doodads, early American portraits of very small children, maybe an Audubon print of a chickadee, French cameos (I have a very nice pair of Donnie and Marie Antoinette), that sort of thing. On the otheur hand, if you have oodles of space, as moi does, you can go for the big stuff, although I would stay away from anything that won't fit in the back of a taxi. Always measure in advance where you plan to put a particular artwork, because unless it's some weird modern thing, if you chop off a piece of a statue it usually looks pretty awful, and you'll be unhappy if, say, you have to cut a hole in a painting to get to the plug thingy when it's time to vacuum.

Once you know what you have space for, all you have to do is go out and poke around and see if you can turn up some dynamite museum pieces. Of course, not everyone knows a high-powered art dealeur like Bernie, but use your noggin. For one thing, you can find out where the artists in your area hang out—it's usually some smoky café that serves pretty odd-tasting coffee, but they often have some nice little pastries, too—and introduce yourself as a patronette of les arts. Artists are easy to spot, with those smocks and silly bow ties and mustaches and funny-looking floppy hats. They always live in grubby little garottes on the tops of old buildings with pigeon doo on the skylights and nothing but a hotplate where they cook awful little cans of stew so they're always hungry and nobody appreciates them, except sometimes the kindly landlady who lets them pay her with paintings, and later she sells them for a bundle and uses the money to pay a lawyer to get her son out of jail where he was sent by mistake for a crime he did not commit. Anyway, you might be able to get some fabulous masterpiece for a mushroom-and-pepperoni pizza, although frankly most of this modern stuff is pretty horrible looking, and you might be better off framing the pizza (Fig. 2).

Another thing you can do is to take out a little ad in the papeur saying something like, "Wanted: Art Masterpieces. Distinguished collecteur on tight budget looking for top-notch art treasures. Please, no pre-1500 paintings with sad-looking people standing in pointy arches with things sticking in their tummies." Or you can go to the shops, which is really the most fun, although I would stay away from those stuck-up antique stores full of a lot of rickety stuff some French king got sick of, and the salespeople give your poodle the fish-eye even though Fou-Fou is very well behaved, and if the little dear takes just one teensy nibble on some stupid tassel, you'd think it was the Smack of Rome by the Frizzigoths. The best spots to find art are those lovely, dim little places just crammed with goodies from floor to ceiling where a teensy bell rings when you open the door, and when you look at a price tag, it doesn't have somebody's zip code on it with a dollar sign in front of it.

As soon as I have discovered something really terrific, I put it to my rigorous test of authenticity. I look closely. Does it have a nice frame? Is it sort of dusty and spideur-webby the way genuine old things always are? Has it got a good, easy-to-read signature you can see from across the room? How about the back—is there perhaps something written there, like a note from the landlady that says "Received from Mr. Cézanne in payment for the rent on garotte #4"? Of course, you can use scientific mumbeau-jumbeau like putting it under an ultra-lavender light, or if, say, it's supposed to be a Rembrandt, testing to make sure it was painted with Dutch Boy paint, but I prefeur to rely on moi's flawless instincts to tell les treaseurs from les turkeys. You also must be careful not to go overboard and reject something wonderful only to find out later that it was the real article. I once found some paint-by-the-numbers markings under a

(Fig. 2) THE SNACK. *Polyurethaned pizza topping on dough. 1984.*

(Fig. 3) Detail of unfinished portion of MONA MOI *found under the frame.*

portrait I got from Bernie, and I thought it was a fake, but he pointed out that the numbers were *roman numerals,* which proved it was at least three hundred years old (Fig. 3)!

Of course, after you have stumbled on a fantastic find, you then have to negotiate with the owneur. The trick here is not to let him know how valuable you think it is. Sort of stroll up to him and say, in an off-le-hand way, "Vous know, I found this dirty old picture over there by that cathedral radio—by the way, I'd say it's Gothique, but I'd have to look at the tubes—and normally I wouldn't touch this thing with a pair of fire tongs, but it does have such a nice frame, and even though it obviously isn't a real Cézanne, in spite of that note on the back, it has a certain authentulosity that has sort of grabbed my very expert eye—I am a graduate of the Hudson River School, as you may or may not know—and there is this teensy bare place over the mantel where it would fit per-fectly, and how much is it?" At this point, no matter what price he names, scream politely, "Are you out of your mind?" and get down to the hard bargaining.

And last, but not le least, after you take an artwork home and put it up, you must be prepared to go to le wall to defend it, because, sad de say, the world is full of bozeaus. Knowing someone like Bernie is a real plus, since he has so many facts at his fingeurtips. I remember when some dolt remarked that my Rodin couldn't be by Rodin because he was born in 1840, and he would have been 143 years old when he sculptulated it, but Bernie happened to know that the year has been devalued in France, and it's worth only seven months now, so Rodin was only seventy-six! In extreme cases, you may find it useful to have a cheap, old dime-store painting around so you can inquire of the annoying creep if he would like to be in a painting, and then when he says yes, pick it up and bash him over the head with it.

One cannot pass on all her secrets of a lifetime of collecting in just a few short pages, but I do hope that moi has awakened in vous a love of the fineur things. Art, moi feels, is the ice cream and fudge sauce on the otherwise somewhat boring poundcake of life. It is the yummy chocolate with a cherry center you find once you peel away the drab tinfoil of the day-to-day grind. It is the rich, creamy hollandaise on the itsy-bitsy piece of broccoli, which you have to put there on the plate in order to have the excuse of eating the sauce of existence. It is—well, moi could go on, but I think vous get the drift.

Kissy-kissy!

THE STAFF OF THE KERMITAGE COLLECTION
Set Design and Sculpture:
Bruce Morozko

Costume Design:
Deborah Lombardi

Ha! Photo Studio:
Calista Hendrickson
Lyndon Mosse
Danielle Obinger
Christie Sherman
Dennis Smith
Karl Soderstrom
Mary Strieff

Special thanks to:
Diana "The Smooch" Zadarla
Christine Cooper